Understanding Coding with

PYTHON

Patricia Harris

PowerKiDS press

New York

Published in 2016 by The Rosen Publishing Group, Inc.
29 East 21st Street, New York, NY 10010

First Edition

Editor: Greg Roza
Book Design: Michael J. Flynn

Photo Credits: Cover (girl) © iStockphoto.com/iofoto; cover, pp. 1, 3–24 (coding background) Lukas Rs/Shutterstock.com; p. 5 Monkey Business Images/Shutterstock.com; p. 7 (laptop computer) Kamil Rejczyk/www.flickr.com/photos/kamilrejczyk/14491659448/CC BY 2.0; p. 7 (Scratch GUI) https://commons.wikimedia.org/wiki/File:Scratch_2.0_Screen_Hello_World.png; p. 9 (laptop computer) koosen/Shutterstock.com; p. 11 Thomas Barwick/Iconica/Getty Images; p. 14 Szasz-Fabian Ilka Erika/Shutterstock.com; p. 21 Jupiter Images/Stockbyte/Getty Images.

Cataloging-in-Publication Data

Names: Harris, Patricia G.
Title: Understanding coding with Python / Patricia G. Harris.
Description: New York : PowerKids Press, 2016. | Series: Kids can code | Includes index.
Identifiers: ISBN 9781508144748 (pbk.) | ISBN 9781508144755 (6 pack) | ISBN 9781508144762 (library bound)
Subjects: LCSH: Python (Computer program language)–Juvenile literature. | Computer programming–Juvenile literature.
Classification: LCC QA76.73.P98 H37 2016 | DDC 005.13'3–dc23

Manufactured in the United States of America

CPSIA Compliance Information: Batch #BW16PK: For Further Information contact Rosen Publishing, New York, New York at 1-800-237-9932

Contents

Our Computerized World

Most people use computers at least once a day, whether it's their desktop, laptop, tablet, or mobile phone. However, computers are used in many other products today, including cars, toys, televisions, elevators, kitchen appliances, and much more. With so many computer applications, it's not surprising that coders have many **programming languages** to choose from.

In the past, coding and programming languages were understood by scientists, computer experts, and dedicated hobbyists. However, coding is no longer thought of as an activity for geniuses. In fact, it's possible for anyone, including you, to start coding with any number of understandable programming languages, such as Python. Coding skills can help you make a game, create a webpage, and prepare for a future career.

Knowing how to code, whether it's with Python or another programming language, has become an important skill in our modern world. It's never too early to start coding!

Why Python?

If there are so many programming languages out there, why use Python? Python's creator, Guido van Rossum, wanted to create a language that was easy to use and understand. He based Python on another language called ABC. Van Rossum kept some features, improved other features, and added new features to make a programming language that even novice coders can understand.

Python is a traditional written-code programming language. That means it uses words and special characters to create code. It can have code grouped into **loops** or in other ways. It has some special **modules** built in to help save time and make coding less repetitive. The code that is entered is called the input, and the results displayed on the computer screen are called output.

Breaking the Code

Van Rossum is a big fan of the 1970s British comedy show *Monty Python's Flying Circus*. In fact, that's where the name Python comes from! Python coders are even encouraged to use quotes from the show when coding in Python! Van Rossum said he chose Python because he needed a name that was "short, unique, and slightly mysterious." He also read *Monty Python* scripts while developing the programming language.

Python is a written-code programming language. Other programs, such as Scratch and Hopscotch, use a **graphical** user **interface**, or GUI (GOO-ee).

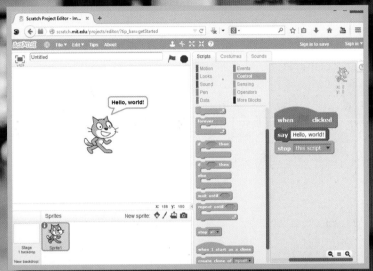

Scratch GUI

Python language

Learn the Rules

Before you can begin to learn about coding in any language, Python included, you need to know that computer programming is about following rules. You might think that sounds a lot like playing a game, and it can be just as much fun.

Rule 1: Coders must know what they want the computer to do and write a plan.

Rule 2: Coders must use special words to have the computer take **input**, make choices, and take action.

Rule 3: Coders need to think about what tasks can be put into a group.

Rule 4: Coders need to use **logic** with AND, OR, NOT, and other logic statements as key words.

Rule 5: Coders must explore the **environment** and understand how it works.

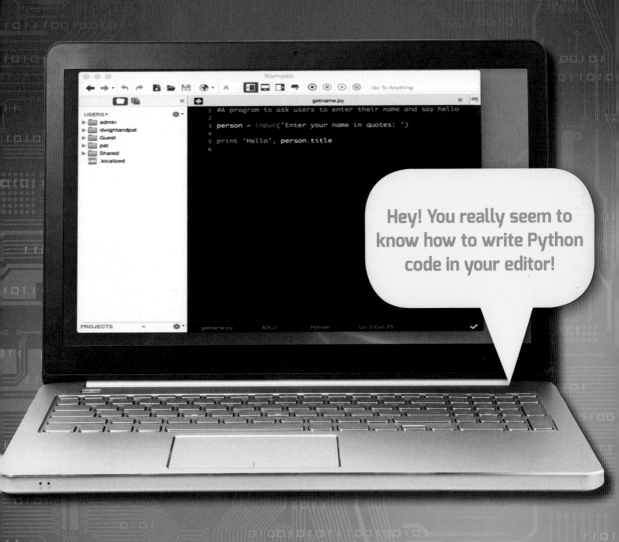

Hey! You really seem to know how to write Python code in your editor!

Breaking the Code

Python is written in a text editor and then run in a **terminal** window on your computer. That means coding with Python is a two-step process. You'll find this process easy once you see how it works.

Print and Display

The **command** "print" means about what it does in English. It displays whatever you've told Python to print on the computer screen. If you want Python to display the number 5, type the code "print 5." Then the output "5" will appear on your screen—it's that easy!

Math operations are built into the Python language. So, to find out the answer to 27 times 43, type the code "print 27*43." Python will then display "1161" on the screen.

If you want the computer to print "Hello!" the code looks like this:

```
print 'Hello!'
```

Notice that the word "Hello" is between single quotes. Python really wants you to use single quotes instead of double quotes almost all the time. The output displayed on the screen is:

```
Hello!
```

A character in Python is anything you type, including letters, quotation marks, and even spaces. Any list of characters that you type between quotation marks in Python is called a string.

Python Environment

Coders must understand the environment in which Python works. You write your programs using a text editor. Most computers come with a text editor installed, but there are many you can download. The text editor allows you to write code, but it doesn't show the results. When you're ready to save the document, name the file and change the **extension** to .py so Python will know it's a Python file.

This is an example of simple lines of Python code in the free text editor Komodo Edit. You can download Komodo Edit from http://komodoide.com/komodo-edit/

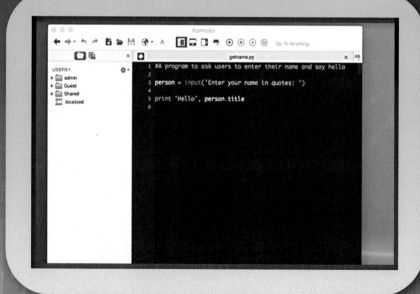

After your program is written and saved, open Python on your computer to see it. On Apple computers, you need to open a terminal window and type in the word "Python," a space, and the name of the program including the .py extension. On PCs, open Python in the Start Menu and type in the file name.

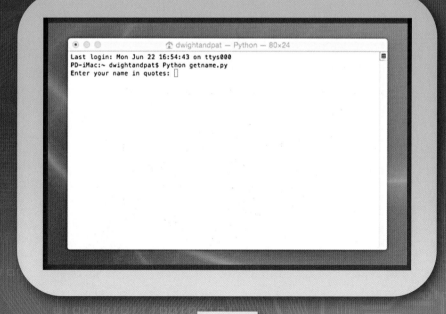

This is the terminal screen on an Apple computer. You can use it to display the results of the Python code you wrote in the text editor.

Hello World!

The first program many programmers write when using a traditional written-code language such as Python is the Hello World program. You must have a plan for every program. The plan is to tell the computer to print to the screen the words "Hello World." This is a simple plan, and the code is also simple.

```
1  # A simple program to print out Hello World
2  print 'Hello World'
```

Notice the first line starts with #. That is the symbol for a comment. For longer comments with several lines, begin with a triple quote (""") and then write your comment. When you're done, type another triple quote on a separate line to close the comment. The pictures show the sample code and the computer output. Notice that you can make this program print more lines just by adding to the program.

```
1   # A simple program to print out Hello World
2   print 'Hello World.'
3   """ I like this program and want to
4   have it say hello again
5   """
6   print 'Hello again, World.'
7
```

```
PD-iMac:~ johndoe$ python helloworld.py
Hello World.
Hello again, World.
PD-iMac:~ johndoe$
```

This is how the terminal displays the code for the Hello World program. Notice no comments appear when the program runs.

Hello Person!

Here's another plan for a Python program: Ask the user to enter his or her name and then print the user a message with the name included. This program requires input from a user. Notice the print command below is specific and tells the users to enter their name in quotes. If they don't use quotes, the program will not get their string. Name your program "getname.py."

```
                            getname.py
1   #A program to ask users to enter their name and say hello
2
3   person = input('Enter your name in quotes: ')
4   print 'Hello', person
5
```

Here is the output for the getname.py program. Notice that name is entered in double quotes. Strings must always be entered in quotes, but numbers are not in quotes.

```
PD-iMac:~ johndoe$ python getname.py
Enter your name in quotes: "Jane"
Hello Jane
PD-iMac:~ johndoe$
```

Let's try a harder program. The code for nameage.py shows input for a name and an age. Notice in the output below that the input for the name is in quotes and the input for age, a number, is not.

```
                                nameage.py
1   person = input('Enter your name in quotes: ')
2   print 'Hello,' + person
3   age = input('Please enter your age with no quotes: ')
4   print 'Hi again,' + person +'!I see you are',age, 'years old.'
5
```

```
PD-iMac:~ johndoe$ python nameage.py
Enter your name in quotes: "Jane"
Hello Jane
Please enter your age with no quotes: 10
Hi again, Jane! I see you are 10 years old.
PD-iMac:~ johndoe$
```

Breaking the Code

Coders can use a program already written and add new commands. That makes coding quicker. Usually they save the new program that's under a new file name so they have the original program and the new one.

17

Here Comes the Turtle

Python Turtle lets you see graphic results. Turtle is a module in Python. You type commands and watch the turtle draw the commands in a special window. Think of the turtle as a robot you control. Turtle helps you begin to think about the special sentence structure and indentation needed in Python. It's also fun!

You have to call the special module at the start of your program. This program requires the use of loops and **variables**. "Length" in the code at right is an example of a variable, because it can be replaced by different numbers.

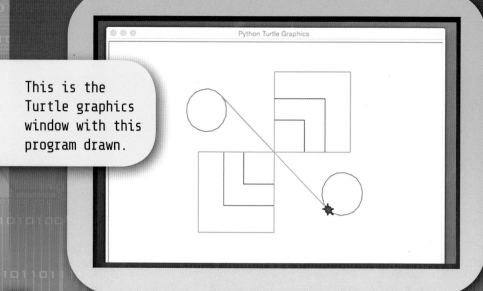

This is the Turtle graphics window with this program drawn.

```
 1   from turtle import *
 2
 3   shape("turtle")
 4
 5   color('blue')
 6   def square(length):
 7       for i in range (0, 4):
 8           forward(length)
 9           left(90)
10
11   square(60)
12   color('red')
13   square(100)
14   color('green')
15   square(150)
16
17   right(180)
18   color('blue')
19   square(60)
20   color('red')
21   square(100)
22   color('green')
23   square(150)
24
25   right(45)
26   forward(150)
27   color('purple')
28   circle(40)
29   color('green')
30   back(180)
31   color('purple')
32   right(180)
33   circle(180)
34
35   done()
```

Calls up the special turtle module (notice *).

Sets the cursor to a turtle shape.

Turtle will draw in blue.

A loop going four times—square is the name of this group. Square is not a built-in command.

Calling the loop to make a square and changing the color and size and calling it again.

Going in a new direction.

Calling the loop again.

Making a line and circles. (Circle is a built-in command.)

Keep your graphics window open so you can see your work.

19

One Step at a Time

By now, you can probably see that coding isn't just for scientists, computer experts, and geniuses. Anyone can code, especially with a language like Python. Once you have a plan and understand some special commands, you can start coding.

Here's a helpful list of steps to get you coding with Python in no time!

1. Write a simple plan. Think about how parts can be grouped.
2. Open your text editor.
3. Write a comment to tell what the program will do.
4. Save your work with the extension .py. Be sure the text editor put the program in your home directory.
5. Start writing code to fit your plan.
6. Add comments in your program whenever you are going to do a new action. Comments will help you remember what's happening.
7. Save your program as you go along and when you think you're finished.
8. On an Apple computer, open the terminal window. At the prompt, type in "python yourfilename.py".
9. On a PC, open Python in the Start menu, then open your file.
10. Run your program with a friend and enjoy!

Using Python is fun! However, it can also help you learn the basics of coding, allowing you to move on to more complex programming languages.

21

Some Python Commands

COMMAND	WHAT IT DOES	EXAMPLES
Print	Displays numbers, math output, or text to screen.	print (25+34)*2 print 'Hello'
#	Starts a one-line comment.	#single-line comment
""" ending on a separate line with """	Prints a comment over several lines.	"""Sometimes it takes several lines for a comment """
variable = input ()	Allows the user to put in data that is requested.	person = input ('Enter your age') [person is the variable that will hold the number typed in]

def variable	Lets you set a word or letter equal to something else.	def square (length)
		    for i in range (0,4):
		    forward(length)
		    left (90)
		[square is the word defined]

If variable = number or string : print 'string'	Tests if a statement is true or false and takes the action included if true or moves to the next program step.	>>> age = 10
		>>> if age < 20 : print ("young")
		...

If variable:
    print 'string'
else:
    print 'string'
	Tests if a statement is true or false, but if the answer is false, takes the action that follows "else:".	>>> age=10
		>>> if age:
		... print "yes"
		... else:
		... print "no"
		...

Glossary

command: A code or message that tells a computer to do something.

environment: The combination of computer hardware and software that allows a user to perform various tasks.

extension: The letters after a dot at the end of a file name that tell what kind of program will open it.

graphical: Having to do with graphics, or pictures and shapes.

interface: A system that allows two things, such as a person and a computer, to communicate with each other.

logic: A proper or reasonable way of thinking about or understanding something.

loop: A process that starts over once it reaches the end.

module: A Python file with a premade set of functions that can be saved and used to save time while coding.

programming language: A coding language designed to give instructions to a computer.

terminal: A computer screen or window where computer data can be viewed.

variable: In Python code, a storage location to which values can be assigned.

Index

Websites

Due to the changing nature of Internet links, PowerKids Press has developed an online list of websites related to the subject of this book. This site is updated regularly. Please use this link to access the list: www.powerkidslinks.com/kcc/pyth